Portsmouth First

Portsmouth First

• ANTHONY TRIGGS •

HALSGROVE

First published in Great Britain in 1999
Reprinted 2008

British Library Cataloguing in Publication Data

A CIP record for this book is available from the British Library

ISBN 978 1 84114 034 6

HALSGROVE
Halsgrove House
Ryelands Industrial Estate, Bagley Road
Wellington, Somerset TA21 9PZ
Tel: 01823 653777
Fax: 01823 216796
www.halsgrove.com

Printed in Great Britain by The Short Run Press Ltd

CONTENTS

INTRODUCTION

After I was asked by Halsgrove to produce this book of Portsmouth superlatives, I sat down to write a preliminary list, with a slight feeling of apprehension. The question foremost in my mind was: would I have enough material to fill a book? After twenty minutes or so spent with a pad and ballpoint I realised that a completely different question had surfaced: how much should I leave out? The collection had to be about Portsmouth, not necessarily about people, so I decided that some of the elder statesmen of literature would be omitted. Sir Walter Besant and George Meredith both fell by the wayside, and poor old H.G. Wells, who only lived in Portsmouth for a short time and hated every minute of it, was a non-starter. But of course, Conan Doyle did invent Sherlock Holmes in Portsmouth, and although not a native of the town, I have included him. However, I have included some of the more unusual items which will interest residents and visitors alike. The twentieth century in Portsmouth saw more change than any other in history. War and subsequent redevelopment brought a huge change to the face of the city, and progress has been reflected greatly in the general style of living: so different to that of the late Victorians and Edwardians. Now Portsmouth has stepped into the unknown of the twenty-first century with even more change planned for the city. There are plans to completely revamp the city centre area, and the Gunwharf redevelopment is well under way. And to top it all there is the tower. Like it or loathe it the elegant spinnaker design has proved to be a focal point to all visitors. As Portsmouth moves into the new millennium let us hope that the next 100 years will provide an even greater list of superlatives and firsts for a great and historic city.

Anthony Triggs
Portchester.

ACKNOWLEDGEMENTS

In putting together a book of this wide-ranging interest I have had to enlist the help of a number of friends, all of whom have given their help and advice willingly: Ron Brown; Dave Garvey; Carole Farr; Stuart Farr; June Long; David Lee curator of the Wessex Film and Sound Archive, Winchester; Carrie Wiltshire, assistant curator of toys, media, and film at Brighton and Hove Museum, Sussex; Captain Jeremy Howard, director of the Marine Society; Judy Burg of the Boots company archive, Nottingham; Susan Harvey, parish secretary of the Anglican Parish of Busselton-Dunsborough, Western Australia; Sherlock Holmes expert Cmdr Geoffrey Stavert; Neil Somerville, senior document assistant at the BBC Written Archives Centre, Caversham; cycling supremo Chris Davies; Mick Cooper; Gerard Blair; Alan King and the staff of the local studies department at the Norrish Central Library, Portsmouth; Brian Sutton; Jeff Legg; Patricia Moore, research librarian at the Library of South Australia, Adelaide; the National Film and Television Archive; and of course Sue whose encouragement is always there.

THE RIGHT PRESCRIPTION

In 1968 the pharmacy and household goods giant Boots finally bought out its greatest rival. In a deal worth £35m – not a huge figure by today's standards – the Nottingham company took over the 622 Timothy Whites and Taylors shops, and within a few years a name known to everyone had disappeared from the High Streets of Britain. What is not so widely known, however, is that the Timothy Whites empire had its humble origins in Portsmouth. Timothy White himself opened his first shop, an oil and dry-saltery business, in Portsea in 1848. He gradually extended his range to include a large variety of household essentials, and soon

The window display is packed with household goods in Timothy White's store in Russell Street in 1938 (Boots archive).

the business increased and new property was acquired. The company's warehouse was established in Chandos Street, and soon after a branch opened its doors in Palmerston Road, Southsea. The Southsea area later became a fashionable and thriving shopping centre, and Timothy White's foresight obviously paid off. By 1904 branches had been opened in the Isle of Wight, Chichester, and Petersfield and the business was formed into a private limited company. After the First World War vigorous expansion followed and the business spread to Kent, Surrey, Devon, Cornwall, Dorset and Somerset. In 1935 Timothy Whites took over the Leeds-based chemist shop chain, Taylors, which added between 500 and 600 small branches to the empire, and led to the company name being changed to Timothy Whites and Taylors. Again more expansion followed with the acquisition of 187 branches of the Mence-Smith Housewares chain in 1944. Timothy White himself died in 1908 aged 84 after retiring to Norfolk. In his time he was the oldest trustee of St John's Church, Portsea; was chief supporter of the Landport Free Ragged Schools; and was a pioneer of the volunteer movement in Portsmouth, retiring from the 2nd Hants Artillery Volunteers with the honorary rank of major. The business, with its slogan, 'It's a pleasure to shop at Timothy Whites and Taylors,' was continued by his son Woolmer, who was a qualified druggist and chemist, and was later knighted for his public services.

MARATHON AT 12 MILES PER HOUR

The motor car was only a few years old when Portsmouth took the lead and became the finishing point for what is thought to be the first road race from London to the south coast. The newly-formed Automobile Club decided to undertake this marathon journey to celebrate four years since the passing of the Locomotives on Highways Act of 1896. On Sunday 12 November, 1900, at 9.30am, 140 vehicles started at Whitehall, at the legal speed of not more than 12 miles per hour. Hundreds of spectators cheered the cars as they arrived at Portsdown Hill, and in Portsmouth thousands packed the streets as the cars drove in procession around the town. It was said that at Kingston Cross people were standing ten deep to get a view of the parade. In the evening a huge banquet was held at the Esplanade Hotel, Southsea presided over by the Mayor of Portsmouth, Alderman A. Emanuel. He praised the winners, and sympathised with the 'also-rans' one of whom was driving a car of his own design. And his name – Charles Rolls!

TRAMWAY TO THE STATUTE BOOK

When a Portsmouth company went into the tramway business it made legal history by having a private act passed through parliament, the first Statutory Tramway Undertaking in the country. The act was dated 8 June 1865 and was entitled: 'An Act for making a Tramway in the Parish of Portsea in the County of Southampton, and for other purposes.' This act enabled the Landport and Southsea Tramway Company to provide an uninterrupted service until trams were discontinued in 1936.

Portsmouth's tram system was one of the earliest in the country.

SWASHBUCKLING SCENARIO

In Broad Street, Old Portsmouth, there once stood a hostelry called the Old Blue Posts. It stood on the site of an even older inn of roughly the same name – the Blue Posts, which was built in 1613 and was destroyed by fire in 1870. The original Blue Posts could be called the cradle of swashbuckling, for it featured strongly in the seafaring adventures penned by Captain Frederick Marryat. Marryat wrote: 'This is the Blue Postesses, Where midshipman leave the chestesses, Call for tea and toastesses, And forget to pay for their breakfastesses.' 'A noted spot was Point,' he also wrote. 'There stood the inviting Blue Posts where many a hungry reefer has enjoyed his tea for two and toast for six. Oh, it was a delectable sight to witness the eagerness with which the

The Old Blue Posts in Broad Street, Old Portsmouth, which replaced the earlier inn made famous by Marryat.

young gentlemen regaled themselves, damning the waiters to show that they were real officers and topping the grandee in extraordinary style, without the least fear of being brought up standing by the first lieutenant.' Marryat himself was of Huguenot descent. He joined the navy as a midshipman in 1806, and left Spithead to spend his first winter at sea in the stormy waters of the Bay of Biscay. By 1812 he was promoted to lieutenant, and made commander by 1815 after serving in various stations throughout the world. He was also an accomplished scientist. He adapted an existing code of signals for merchant vessels which came into general use throughout the world and brought him membership of the Royal Society in 1817. He had an interest in lifesaving, and invented a lifeboat which led to a gold medal from the Royal Humane Society. However it was his writing which brought him lasting fame. The adventures based on his own experiences stirred the imagination of readers and brought the romance of the south coast to a worldwide audience. In 1829 while serving aboard the frigate *Ariadne* he wrote a three-volume novel called *The Naval Officer*. He received an immediate payment of £400 and the book soon became a literary and financial success. He found the manuscript of *The King's Own*, an earlier book he had written, dusted it off, and it was published a year later. Marryat resigned his command in 1830 and settled down to a literary career publishing more novels including *Mr Midshipman Easy* and *Peter Simple*. He later turned to writing books for children, two of which, *Masterman Ready* and *Children of the New Forest*, are the best known. He died in 1848 after learning of the death of his eldest son Frederick aboard the paddle frigate *Avenger* off the coast of Africa. Marryat's stories continue to be popular, and at the time of writing a

Swashbuckling author Captain Frederick Marryat.

dramatisation of his *Children of the New Forest* was showing on BBC television. The Old Blue Posts may be gone, but the memories linger on in Marryat's stirring descriptions of nineteenth-century naval life.

THERE'S NO CASE LIKE HOLMES

The year is 1887 and an impecunious young Scottish doctor, now resident in Southsea, is whiling away the hours waiting for patients by putting pen to paper. At his surgery at Bush House, Elm Grove, he is writing a short story with the hope of making a few pounds to supplement his meagre income. Eventually the tale is finished and he sends it off to various magazines, with, sadly, little success. The *Cornhill Magazine*, a leading short-story paper, describes it as a 'shilling dreadful,' and returns it speedily. Publishers Ward Lock, however, agree to take it for their *Beeton's Christmas Annual*, edited by Samuel Beeton, the husband of Mrs Beeton of cookery book fame. They offer the young doctor £25 outright for the copyright, and although he would rather have a royalty agreement, the author accepts. The story, *A Study in Scarlet*, appears in the 1887 edition of the magazine. Thus was one of the most enduring characters of British fiction thrust upon the reading public, for the author's name was Arthur Conan Doyle, and the hero was, of course, the world's first consulting detective, Sherlock Holmes. At the time this publishing event passed with hardly a flutter in the literary world, but by now Conan Doyle had found an agent, A.P. Watt, who sent two more stories to H. Greenhough Smith at the *Strand Magazine*. The doctor was offered £200 for six, and success was imminent. Conan Doyle was later to write: 'It struck me that a single character running through a series – if it engaged the attention of the reader – would bind the reader to the particular magazine.' How right he was! A further offer of £300 for another six tales sparked Conan Doyle to give

Conan Doyle's first consulting rooms were in Bush House, squeezed in next to the Bush Hotel.

up his practice and set up as a freelance writer, and the rest – as they say – is history. During his time at Portsmouth Conan Doyle involved himself firmly in the community. He was a member of the Portsmouth Literary and Scientific Society, was a keen photographer, and played in goal for the embryonic Portsmouth Football Club. Bush House was destroyed in the Second World War, and now a block of flats occupies the site. A plaque commemorating the centenary of the 'birth' of the great detective was unveiled on 18 November, 1982, by the then secretary of the Sherlock Holmes Society of London, Capt. William Mitchell – who was himself born in Portsmouth – and the chairman of the city council libaries, museums and arts committee, Councillor Les Kitchen.

Sir Arthur Conan Doyle.

Flashback to 1982 and the plaque is unveiled by Capt. William Mitchell, left, and Councillor Les Kitchen.

TOP OF THE TABLE

Although the game of billiards had been played in various forms since the sixteenth century, it took on a whole new popularity in late Victorian times. This was mainly due to a number of talented professionals who perfected their skills and played tournaments and exhibition matches at various venues around the country, drawing huge audiences. Most gentlemen's clubs had billiards rooms, there were many public halls, and most affluent Victorians would have a table in their homes, so the young men of the day had every opportunity to emulate their idols. Although the ladies played, it was obvious from articles in contemporary magazines that they were there just to add that bit of glamour, and were not to be taken seriously. That was until Portsmouth girl Eva Collins came on the scene. Eva was the younger daughter of professional billiards player George Collins, she knew the game inside out, brought competitiveness to the ladies' game, and eventually became lady billiards champion of the world. Little Eva stood barely 4ft 6in in her high buttoned boots, and she had to mount a stool to use the long rest, but for all that she was a top performer. In October 1897 billiards champion and entrepreneur John Roberts introduced the first public tournament featuring lady players. It was held at the Egyptian Hall, Piccadilly, London, with the teenage Eva taking on Grace Fairweather. Although Eva lost the match, it nevertheless put her on the road to professional success. She frequently played exhibition matches in Portsmouth, and at one time she played before an audience of 200 petty officers at the Royal Naval Barracks. She was also a golfer and swimmer of great prowess, and was a skilled musician. Eva maintained her association with the game until late in life, and in her late sixties she played against several men at a holiday camp and astonished them by winning every game. The love of the green baize table didn't stop with Eva and her father. Her elder sister Laura was a billiards player of some proficiency, and was good enough to become the instructress at the Ladies' Lyceum Club at Piccadilly. In 1961 Eva retired from her job with Britain's leading firm of billiards room fitters, having risen to the heights of her sport.

In this rare picture Eva Collins prepares to wipe the smirk from the faces of her male opponents.

FLOATING INTO HISTORY

To serve the huge battleships that were frequently to be seen in Portsmouth, a huge floating dock was commissioned – not just a big one, but the biggest in the world. This sea-going juggernaut was ordered in 1909, and Harland and Wolff delivered it to Portsmouth in August 1912, where it was a familiar sight until 1939 after which it was towed away for service in Malta. The huge structure covered an area of more than two acres and boasted a lifting capacity of 40,000 tons, which could raise the largest warship afloat at that time. In order that repair materials for ships could be brought alongside the floating dock a £100,000 railway jetty was built at Fountain Lake in the dockyard.

The huge floating dock sits in the harbour awaiting a warship for repairs.

LEADERS IN LINGERIE

In 1912 the woman's correspondent of the *Evening News* wrote: 'There is no reason why Portsmouth should not rival Paris, if the women of Portsmouth will only imitate the Parisiennes and have a care for their corsets. For fifty years Portsmouth has been the hub of the corset trade in the United Kingdom, and never was its prosperity so marked as it is today.' The French sentiments may be doubtful, but there is no doubt that Portsmouth led the world in the production of corsets, and later, every other form of ladies' underwear you can imagine. Back in the days before naval allottments, seafarers' wives had to find their own ways of surviving while their men were away at sea – often for years at a time, rather than months. It didn't take the manufacturers of naval uniforms long to realise there was a huge untapped workforce out there in the town, and the more simple jobs such as sewing shirts, were soon being passed out to the naval wives. In fact shirt manufacturing persisted in Portsmouth until fairly recently. However it was the makers of stays – the forerunners of corsets – who really jumped on the bandwagon, and by the mid 1800s there were as many as 4000 women employed by a handful of manufacturers. Such names as Helby, Fletcher, Bowden, Bayer, Izod, Perrins, Alder, and Vollers of Kingston Road all had workshops producing undergarments for thousands of outlets across the country. By the 1920s the range of items increased, and soon corsets were taking second place to other items of lingerie, and by the 1960s some of the best names in ladies' underwear were being produced by the Portsmouth factories. Two of the larger companies, Chilcot and Williams, and Leethems – with their Twilfit range – continued to lead the field, at one time the latter company having five factories around the city. Now, sadly the industry is no more. Although the Kingson Road shop premises are closed, Vollers still continue in business, enjoying a revival thanks to the recent spate of period films and TV dramas and pop star Madonna's prediliction for wearing corsets on stage, while Tipner lingerie manufacturer Murphys, which was facing closure, has been bought by the Anne Summers company, promising a brighter future for its employees. And that is the final link to a Portsmouth industry that has cossetted, squeezed, shaped and uplifted women from all over the world.

The Vollers shop in Kingston Road in the days when corsets were a necessity.

Workers at Leethem's Twilfit Marina factory in Highland Road at Portsmouth.

GRAVES OF THE GREAT

A grave in Highland Cemetery marks the resting place of a man of valour. He was Henry James Raby, a veteran of Crimea, and the first man ever to be awarded the Victoria Cross, the decoration for bravery introduced by Queen Victoria in 1856. This fact alone is of historical importance, but in addition the cemetery contains the greatest number of VC holders in the world. Altogether eight decorated heroes – two more from the first investiture – are buried in the graveyard. Henry Raby was a Royal Navy commander and his bravery in rescuing an injured soldier while under heavy fire at Sebastopol in 1855, resulted in the Victoria Cross award. He was first on the list to be awarded the decoration at the very first investiture of the VC at Hyde Park on 26 June, 1857. Fifth on the list, and also buried at Highland cemetery, was Lieutenant William Hewett, who was with the naval brigade at Inkerman. He disregarded an order to stop and retire from a hopeless position. Hewett replied: 'Retire? Retire be damned!' and proceeded to shoot his way out of trouble. When he died in Haslar Hospital, at Gosport in 1888, Queen Victoria sent a wreath. Nearby is John Robarts, who also received the award at the first investiture ceremony, and who won the VC for risking his life to set fire to enemy stores in the Crimea. Gunner Israel Harding, naval lieutenant Hugh Cochrane, Surgeon Lieutenant Colonel William Temple, and Lieutenant Hugh Shaw take the number to seven. The eighth VC holder is Lance Corporal William Goat, who won his medal in the Indian Mutiny on 6 March 1858 at Lucknow. He was with the 9th Lancers when he rescued the body of his major without fear for his own life. He died in Leopold Street at the age of sixty four and was buried in the cemetery, possibly in a shared grave with no mention on the headstone. Also in the graveyard at Highland Road is Mrs George Fox who was awarded the Order of the Royal Red Cross. She died in Cambridge Barracks, Portsmouth, in 1888 from injuries suffered in the Transvaal, and was afforded full military

William Hewett shoots his way out of trouble, as portrayed in the Illustrated London News *of 13 July, 1861.*

The grave of Admiral Sir William Hewitt in Highland Cemetery.

honours at her funeral. There are other Victoria Cross connections with the city. Today part of the city's ferry port covers what once was Mile End Cemetery, formerly the Portsea Island General Cemetery where another man of valour rests. On 5 November, 1854, naval rating Thomas Reeves was supporting the army's Right Lancaster Battery at the Battle of Inkerman in 1854 and came under sustained attack by Russian forces. While numerous soldiers were cut down, Seaman Reeves and two naval colleagues, John Gorman and Mark Scholefield, managed to repel the attack, handing down their muskets to injured soldiers to reload. For the heroic defence of their position, forcing back the Russians against the odds, all three men were awarded the Victoria Cross, and received the medals at the first investiture.

HIGH-FLYING CITY

Portsmouth entered the air age in 1932 after the city fathers decided in their wisdom that flying was the travel of the future. Portsmouth wasn't the first municipal airport to be opened, but according to the country's leading aviator, it was certainly the best. Blackpool, Hull, Norwich, Liverpool, Nottingham, Manchester, and Bristol had all applied for civil airport licences, and it was this fact that galvanised

Crowds gather around the unusual Westland-Hill Pterodactyl aircraft at the airport opening day.

the council into action. Seventy-six acres of land at Highgrove were purchased and cleared, and the 204-acre airport began to take shape. It was opened in July 1932 with great pageantry, an air display, and a controversial visit from the Graf Zeppelin. Air ace Sir Alan Cobham brought his famous flying circus to Portsmouth a week later on National Aviation Day, and put the airport in the top spot by saying: 'It is the best aerodrome I have landed in.' These words were reinforced in September of 1936 when the airport was chosen for the start of the air race to Johannesburg because of its 'billiard table' surface, and its ability to get the aircraft into the air at one-minute intervals. Sadly no one could have foreseen the great strides that would be taken in air travel after the war, and the pocket handkerchief airport with its grass runways was unable to compete and ultimately closed.

Aviator Sir Alan Cobham pictured on one of a set of popular cigarette cards produced by Lambert and Butler.

FUEL IN FLIGHT

Today the world is a smaller place, thanks to air travel. We think nothing of taking a long-haul holiday, when the huge jet makes a nine or ten-hour journey non-stop without refuelling. And films and television often show fighter planes taking on fuel in the air from huge tanker aircraft, with the long hose locking on to the nose pick-up, a technique which was perfected in Portsmouth. One of the directors of aircraft manufacturer Airspeed, which moved to the city from York in 1933, was Sir Alan Cobham, and he was planning to enter a plane in the Australia endurance bid. Together with Squadron Leader W. Helmore he worked towards developing a viable flight refuelling system to give the plane, an Airspeed Courier, a greater operating range. A huge Handley Page W10, normally used in Cobham's Flying Circus, was stripped of its seating and a track was built inside. Fuel drums were rolled down the track and the one at the tail end of the fuselage was connected to a hose, which in turn was connected to a trailing rope. The Courier had been specially modified to provide a large hatch in the cabin top. After the two aircraft had taken off, and the Courier was about 50ft below and astern of the tanker, Helmore would stand up in the hatch and grab the trailing rope – which was levelled in flight by a child's balloon filled with water – to haul in the hose and connect it to the fuel tank. Time and time again the two men undertook this dangerous exercise until it was honed down to a fine art. By 1934 the endurance

The Airspeed Courier positions itself astern of the big Handley Page ready to take on fuel.

Squadron Leader Helmore reaches out through the Courier's hatch to grab the trailing rope.

flight had been rescheduled to finish in India. Cobham took off on 21 September, and the first transfer of fuel was effected over Selsey Bill. The Courier continued to Malta where a second transfer took place. At that point Cobham discovered that the throttle control was no longer working and there was no option but to make an emergency landing, grossly overloaded with fuel, at Halfar. The throttle problem was found to be a faulty split pin in the mechanism. However before the Courier could take off again on its long onward flight Cobham learned of a tragedy. Back in England the Handley Page had crashed on its way to Coventry for a National Aviation Day display, killing the crew, and Cobham had no alternative but to abandon the flight. However the air-to-air method had proved its worth and was gradually improved upon. Later a separate company was formed, Flight Refuelling Ltd, which has continued into the supersonic age. But this technique owes its success to primitive manouevres carried out in the skies over Portsmouth.

TEACHING THE POOR

In this enlightened age education is available to all, but in early Victorian times it was an expensive privilege. Without money any form of education was an impossibility and among the desperately-poor classes children would invariably turn to theft or prostitution just to stay alive. It was the Ragged Schools movement, started in the 1840s, that gave poor and destitute children to opportunity to gain a rudimentary education, which would give them a small advantage to make a better life for themselves. In 1844 the Seventh Earl of Shaftesbury became the president of the Ragged Schools Union, a philanthropic organisation which eventually became the Shaftesbury Society. But it was the work of a poor Portsmouth cobbler that started the whole movement, leading to a complete rethink on education with the introduction of the welfare state. John Pounds was born on 17 June, 1766, in St Mary's Street, Old Portsmouth. His father was a dockyard carpenter, and when John was twelve he apprenticed him to a shipwright. But tragedy changed the life of the young man. He fell down into a dry dock and fractured his thigh, which crippled him and made him incapable of continuing in the dockyard. The young John Pounds then took an apprenticeship with a shoemaker, and after he finished his time he set up his own boot and shoe repair business in a tiny wooden workshop in Highbury Street. He was never very skilled at his trade, and he always allowed his poor neighbours to pay at their own convenience. After some years he adopted the crippled one-year-old son of his brother. He reared the child and later taught him his trade, and eventually cured the boy's

John Pounds is surrounded by barefoot children in his tiny home.

deformity with home-made surgical boots. The necessity of teaching the lad the basics of reading, writing, botany, and religion, revealed to John that he had a gift for teaching, so he attracted to his workshop illiterate street urchins and began to instill knowledge into them. On most days he would have 30 or 40 youngsters at his shop, many having to sit outside because of the lack of room. After his death in 1839 his good example stimulated others to carry on with his work, not only in Portsmouth but in all parts of the country. John Pounds was buried in the grounds of the former Unitarian Church, now the John Pounds Memorial Church, in High Street, Old Portsmouth, where his memorial can still be seen. At the time of writing the John Pounds of Portsmouth heritage appeal is hoping to raise £40,000 to create a replica of his shop in the grounds of the church. Their appeal was launched on New Year's Day 1999 – exactly 160 years after Pounds's death.

A CRADLE OF COMEDY

A small round plaque high on a wall above a Southsea Chinese restaurant marks the place where a stalwart of British comedy was born. Even if you're too young to remember the zany situations of the *Goon Show* on BBC radio, you must have laughed at the enduring humour of Peter Sellers as Inspector Jacques Clouseau in the Pink Panther movies. Richard Henry Sellers was born on 8 September 1925 in the flat above the shop at what was locally known as Postcard Corner, on the junction of Castle Road and Southsea Terrace. The shop was owned by Hubert Lightbown who specialised in selling postcards, hence the nickname for the junction. Sellers's parents, Bill and Peg, were in show business and were appearing at the Kings Theatre in a revue called *The Vanity Box*, starring the great Will Hay. Bill was a piano player and Peg a dancer. The young Peter joined his parents on stage at an early age, and had won a talent contest by the time he was thirteen. He became a drummer after leaving school, and at seventeen he joined the RAF in the entertainments section as an impressionist. After leaving the service he broke into radio, appearing in such shows as *Show Time*, *It's Fine to be Young*, and *Ray's a Laugh*, before moving on to stardom in the *Goon Show*. Radio appearances led to film roles, and Sellers appeared in a string of 1950s comedy movies, including *The Ladykillers*, *Up The Creek*, and *Two-way Stretch*, before moving on to main feature films. By the close of the decade his popularity was worldwide and in the '60s he developed into a star of international class, working in Hollywood for a great deal of the time. However fame began to take its toll and a number of movie failures and a series of heart attacks in the late '60s affected him badly. Sellers died on 24 July, 1980, leaving a rich legacy of comedy and a Portsmouth memory.

Arch-Goon Peter Sellers in his role as the bumbling Inspector Clouseau from the Pink Panther movies.

The plaque to Peter Sellers above the shop on the corner of Castle Road and Southsea Terrace.

BIG ON BROLLIES

A memorial in Westminster Abbey recalls the first man in the country to carry an umbrella, at least thirty years before the practice came into normal use. However his fame did not stop at this rather unusual habit, but continued into a life of philanthropy and good deeds. Jonas Hanway was born on 12 August 1712 in St George's Square, Portsmouth. He was apprenticed at an early age to a Lisbon merchant, and later moved on to obtain a partnership in a St Petersburg firm, in which capacity he travelled widely, especially in Persia and the far east. He then inherited a fortune and settled down to helping the poor and distressed. He fought to ban child chimney sweeps, campaigned for Sunday schools, but more importantly in 1756 he founded the Marine Society, the world's oldest public maritime charity, which in 1786 commissioned the *Beatty*, the first pre-sea training ship in the world. However this life took its toll on his finances and as some recompense for his life of kindness he was offered the position of navy commissioner for victualling. For twenty years he operated from the Square Tower at Old Portsmouth, after he had converted the old landing stage into a pier – known as the beef stage – to serve the fleet at Spithead. And as for the umbrella – an item which up to that time had only been used by seamstresses to protect their work and by parsons at funerals – it is perhaps understandable that it caused interest. It was of Persian manufacture, light green on the outside and pale pink within. It had a carved handle with a joint in the middle so Hanway could fold it up and put it in the pocket of his coat. Hanway died on 5 September 1786.

Jonas Hanway from a painting in the collection of the Marine Society at its London headquarters. The furniture he is shown using is still in use at the society's headquarters in Lambeth Road, London. (The Marine Society).

BOATS AND BRIDGES

Britain Street was situated just off St George's Square, near the Mill Dam Barracks. It consisted of flat-fronted houses with shallow bay windows so typical of the eighteenth century. However in one of those tiny homes on 9 April 1806 the great engineer Isambard Kingdom Brunel was born. Brunel's father, Marc, was the inventor of the block mills in the dockyard, and the son displayed a similar inventive aptitude. In later life he designed the Clifton Suspension Bridge, Saltash Bridge, the *SS Great Western* – the first regular liner to sail between Britain and America – and the *SS Great Britain*, then the largest ship in the world. The *Great Britain* was 322 feet long and carried 130 crew and 360 passengers, and was the first ever ocean-going propeller driven iron ship. After sterling service she was allowed to decay, but was saved, and like the *Warrior* at Portsmouth, she was brought back to her home port of Bristol where a continuing process of restoration is still going on. Brunel died in 1859 and never saw the completion of his favourite project, the Clifton Suspension Bridge. Today a small plaque on a pillar near the site of Britain Street marks the birthplace of a great builder and dreamer.

The mounted plaque which now marks the approximate location of Brunel's birthplace.

Brunel's birthplace in Britain Street, Portsea.

LOCKSMITH EXTRAORDINARY

A tiny house in Daniel Street, Portsea, long gone since the '30s, marks the spot where a world-wide company – still in existence today – was founded. One night in 1816, it was here that locksmith Jeremiah Chubb dreamed of the way to make a lock that would be impossible to force. He promptly awoke his employee Ebenezer Hunter, together they went to the nearby workshop, and the detector lock was born. The mechanism of the lock made it almost impossible to pick, but also indicated whether an attempt had been made to do so. The detector was patented in 1818 in the names of Jeremiah Chubb and Ebenezer Hunter after interest had been shown it it by the Prince Regent (later George IV) who saw it during a visit to the dockyard. It is recorded that following the appearance of the lock, a convict on board a prison hulk in the harbour, who was by profession a lockmaker, claimed he had picked with ease some of the best mechanisms, and could do the same with the detector lock. He was given all the tools he needed, the promise of £100 from Chubb, and an even more inviting promise of a free pardon from the government if he succeeded. After some months he gave up, and the resulting publicity put the detector lock on the road to success. The invention should have made Jeremiah's fortune, but sadly he drifted into poverty, leaving his elder brother Charles to carry on the company business. Charles, who lived in Queen Street on the corner of Union Street, made improvements to the lock, and in 1824 took out new patents. In 1835 he patented a process intended to make safes fire-proof and burglar-proof, and subsequently moved the company to

Chubb's house in Daniel Street, Portsea.

two new bases – Wolverhampton and London – where he established a huge purpose-built factory. The *National Commercial Directory* of 1830 described him as the 'inventor of the improved detector lock and combination latch – lock manufacturer to His Majesty, to HRH the Duke of Cambridge, the Board of Ordnance, the Navy Board, and the governor and company of the Bank of England.' Charles died in 1845 and was succeeded by his son John, who was himself a clever craftsman. In 1848 he invented a railway safe fitted with a revolving door access, of a type which now feature in banks' night safes. The family retained its connections with Portsmouth for many years with Charles Hayter Chubb sponsoring fund-raising for the Duchess of Albany's home for ex-servicemen in the city. The company is still a great force in the world of security, but it all started in that little house in Daniel Street.

The modern-looking Chubb factory in London in 1868.

TAKING THE CUP

The 17 May 2008 saw a great FA Cup victory for Portsmouth. But on 29 April, 1939, the Guildhall Square was a seething mass of humanity. People had climbed on to the roofs of buildings and up lamp posts to obtain a good view of the events. What was it all about? Earlier that day Pompey's greatest victory to date had taken place when they took the FA Cup at Wembley with a 4-1 victory over Wolverhampton Wanderers. The bus brought the victorious team – and the cup – from Fratton station to an unbelievably crowded square, where fans clamoured to get a view of their heroes. But there was another reason why the club went into the record books, and that was determined by the date. On 3 September of that year war with Germany was declared, and the FA cup games were put in mothballs for the duration. So Pompey holds the record for being in possession of the cup for the longest time ever, and without having to score another goal!

Crowds in the Guildhall Square clamour to see the conquering heroes and the all-important FA Cup.

A ROAD'S PREMIER POSITION

As a boy Leonard James Callaghan played in the fields gazing down on Portsmouth. In the 1920s Portsmouth's tower blocks were not dreamed of, but the dockyard cranes and houses shoe-horned into hundreds of narrow streets were familiar to him. And in May 1997 former prime minister Lord Callaghan of Cardiff returned to the same spot on Portsdown Hill to have a road named after him, and in keeping with his popular soubriquet of Sunny Jim he brought a bright day with him too. The Ministry of Defence had no further use for the military road which runs west from the junction of Portsdown Hill Road and Southwick Hill Road, so the city council adopted it. In 1991 Lord Callaghan was made a freeman of Portsmouth and since then the council had been looking for a road to name after one of the city's most famous sons, and so James Callaghan Drive came into being. Lord Callaghan was born in 1912 in a three-bedroom bay-and-forecourt house in Westbourne Road, Copnor. He was educated at Portsmouth Northern Secondary School, was prime minister from 1976-79 and then became leader of the opposition. He was made a life peer in 1987. Now his name will live on high above the city of his birth.

Lord Callaghan, left, with Lady (Audrey) Callaghan and the then Lord Mayor of Portsmouth, Councillor Tony Golds, at the naming of James Callaghan Drive (The News, *Portsmouth*).

REVIEWING THE SITUATION

Over the years the name of Spithead has become synonymous with fleet reviews. Jubilees and other royal celebrations have invariably sparked the huge gathering of Great Britain's naval power, and Portsmouth in welcoming the officers and crews from the multinational collection of warships, has become the review capital of the world. Nowhere in the world could such a continuous

The royal yacht Victoria and Albert *slides magnificently along the lines of warships at the 1937 review.*

The Prince of Wales (later Edward VIII) and George V at Spithead for the 1924 review, pictured on a cigarette card from the patriotic Wills set The Reign of George V.

parade of ships have been possible, and Spithead is forever associated with the long lines of vessels stretching out as far as the eye can see. Back in 1346 Edward III reviewed his fleet before leaving for France, and later, in 1415, Henry V surveyed 1400 ships prior to leaving for the continent and the battle of Agincourt. Through the centuries the number of vessels increased until the golden age of Queen Victoria, when Britain's naval might was at its greatest. From Victoria's first review on 1 March, 1842, until 1 February, 1901, with the homage review after her death, there were as many as 17 naval events at Spithead. These included the grand naval review in 1853, the Golden Jubilee review in 1887, and the Diamond Jubilee review in 1897. After Victoria's death a number of other fleet reviews were held, notably those for the various coronations – Edward VII in 1902, George V in 1911, George VI in 1937, and our present queen in 1953 – culminating in Her Majesty's Silver Jubilee review in 1977 (the first to include nuclear-powered ships and submarines) which brings up to date a Portsmouth tradition stretching back for more than 600 years.

FROM FILMS TO FLOWERS

Thomas Edison is generally considered to be the inventor of the cinematographic process, eventually leading to the cinema we know today. However, while he was busy with his process in the United States, enthusiasts here in the United Kingdom were conducting their own experiments, and one of the earliest of these was a Portsmouth man. Alfred John West was a professional photographer with a keen interest in maritime subjects. He was quick to perceive the link between apparent movement and single-frame photography and early on in his career he developed an instantaneous shutter which enabled him to produce

The freemasons make their way to St Matthew's church, shown in a frame from West's historic film.

moving pictures, possibly putting him in the forefront of British cinematography. On 8 June, 1898, the Duke of York (later George V) sailed in command of the Portsmouth-built *HMS Crescent*, and Alfred West was aboard to record some of the events. The day before he had recorded activities at the naval base, as reported in the *Hampshire Telegraph*: 'Photographs of naval depot stokers at drill were taken on the parade ground near *HMS Wellington* in Portsmouth dockyard for reproduction by the cinematograph.' After the cruise he set up an impromptu outdoor cinema on the dockside for the *Crescent* officers and crew to see the results. The film, *Our Navy*, became a great success for West, and attracted countrywide interest, and for a number of years it was shown continuously at the Regent Street Polytechnic in London. Queen Victoria became interested, and wishing to see her grandson on the screen, arranged for West to give special showing on Saturday 27 August, 1898, at Osborne House, on the Isle of Wight. In the years before the First World War Alfred West continued producing films. In 1902 he covered a parade of freemasons on their way to the foundation stone ceremony for the now-defunct St Matthew's church. The Revd Bruce Cornford, vicar-designate of St Matthew's, was a prominent freemason, and proud of his life's work in building the church, he commissioned West to film the ceremony. The Church of the Holy Spirit church council held the cine film until recently when it was

Film-maker extraordinary Alfred West.

donated to the Wessex Film and Sound Archive at Winchester, where it is thought to be the oldest piece of movie film in existence. The archive now has about half a dozen West films in its collection. Just before the First World War West took an extended trip to Australia, and on his return he decided the film business had become too much for him: he was, after all, in his late fifties. He sold up and bought a small farm in the Isle of Wight where he started a new business cultivating violets, another successful enterprise. He returned to Portsmouth after the death of his wife and took a house in Wimbledon Park Road, where he lived until his death in 1937. His obituary in the *Evening News* described him as 'the grandfather of the films,' a fitting accolade for a man who was an acknowledged leader in the world of motion pictures.

AGE NO HANDICAP TO DUTY

On 9 November, 1907, an unusual chapter was added to Great Britain's municipal history. In Portsmouth town hall the council invested Doris Foster with a glittering badge of office, and she became the nation's youngest mayoress at the age of five and a half. For the little girl the ceremony must have been an emotional experience. Her mother had died a short time previously, and her father, Councillor Ferdinand Foster, had accepted the mayoralty only under pressure from a united town council. Applauding the decision, the *Evening News* commented: 'The place of the motherless daughter is by her father's side, and although it cannot be expected that a little maid of this tender age can preside over many functions, there will be occasions to which her presence will lend additional attraction and will ensure more generous effort than could be expected in ordinary circumstances.' This prediction proved to be soundly based. Little Doris was to play a notable part in sustaining one of the chief charitable efforts of the mayoral year – the endowment of two cots in the children's ward of the Royal Portsmouth Hospital. The children of Portsmouth rallied to the call of the little mayoress, and the proceeds from concerts they staged helped to boost the fund. Five days after assuming office, Doris stood beside her father to help in receiving guests at a town hall reception in honour of the German naval officers whose ships had escorted Kaiser Wilhelm to Portsmouth in his royal yacht. It was a glittering occasion with much heel-clicking as the bemedalled visitors bowed over Doris's tiny hand. Throughout her year the little mayoress was present at a

Young Doris Foster, mayoress extraordinary.

huge array of notable opening occasions – that of Copnor Bridge, the rebuilt South Parade Pier, and the new municipal college. In 1908, in a bid to make the hospital a little less frightening for the children, three murals made of Doulton tiles and depicting Biblical subjects were fixed to the walls of the new children's ward at the Royal Portsmouth Hospital prior to the official opening by Princess Helena Victoria the following year. One commemorated little Doris's successful end to her year. She raised £1000 for the cot fund, and it is perhaps appropriate that the design depicted a quotation from Isiah, chapter 11: 'A little child shall lead them.' Later, in 1932, three more panels were added, this time featuring nursery rhymes. When the hospital was eventually demolished these beautiful murals were saved and can be seen in the stairway of the city museum, one recalling the little girl who made civic history.

The Doulton tile panel recalling child mayoress Doris Foster.

ADDRESSING THE MATTER

Postcodes today speed our mail, but letters addressed to one famous Portsmouth resident had no trouble in reaching their destination. The great maritime painter W. H. Wyllie lived at No 1 Tower House, Old Portsmouth, and he utilised the old tramways stables building for his studio. The address of the studio was unique – it was the only address in the world which could not be copied – for on the archway

Marine artist W. H. Wyllie.

was inscribed the building's exact latitude and longitude. The Post Office delivered many letters addressed to: Mr Wyllie, Lat 50° 47' 25" North – Long 1° 6' 25" West. Although the building was badly damaged during the war the archway can still be seen today. Wyllie painted seascapes and naval battle scenes, and his panorama of Trafalgar was presented to the nation and can be seen in the Royal Naval Museum at the historic dockyard. Wyllie was held in such esteem that the navy accorded him full naval honours at his funeral on 6 April, 1931. He and his wife are buried in St Mary's church, within the grounds of Portchester Castle.

The old tramways stables building with its distinctive arch is pictured in pre-war days.

DEMISE OF DUELLING

The last fatal duel in England – the duel that presaged the end of duelling in this country – was fought in 1845 over the matter of protecting the honour of a Portsmouth woman. And although the actual meeting took place on the Gosport side of the harbour – at Browndown – the events leading up to it were sparked in Portsmouth town. The King's Rooms on the seafront at Southsea, run by Henry Hollingsworth, was a popular meeting place for the young bloods and junior officers of Southsea's early Victorian society. Featuring elegant suites, ballrooms and lounges, the rooms had been opened in 1816 and were named to commemorate the visit to the town of William IV. But at a soiree on the evening of 19 May, 1845, trouble was brewing on the glittering dance floor. For some weeks a young married Dragoons officer, Captain James Seton, had seemingly been paying rather too much attention to Isabella, the beautiful wife of Royal Marines officer, Lieutenant Henry Hawkey. The situation came to a head on that spring evening when Hawkey, an irascible man at the best of times, called Seton into a private room and demanded satisfaction, failing which he would publicly horse-whip him in the High Street. Seton's insolent reply caused Hawkey to lose control and he delivered a well-aimed boot to the seat of the young Dragoon's neatly-pressed trousers. Duelling was illegal, but in the armed services honour was paramount, so the two men arranged to meet at Browndown at teatime the next day. It is perhaps easy to feel sympathy for Seton, who by this time was undoubtedly wondering how his philandering had led him to this course of action. Not so Hawkey. He had bought a pair of duelling pistols for £10 and spent the morning at a shooting gallery brushing up on his skills. Teatime saw the pair at Browndown with their young seconds – both under the age of twenty – where they each took the regulation fifteen paces, turned and faced each other. Seton fired first and missed, leaving Hawkey time to aim, but his gun misfired. At that point the encounter should have ended with honour satisfied, but the inexperienced seconds allowed the pistols to be reloaded and Marine and Dragoon faced one another for a second time. Seton again missed, but Hawkey's ball found its mark, hitting the young Dragoon in the lower belly, near the right hip. Hawkey and his second, Lieutenant Henry Pym, hurriedly left, and it was left to Seton's second, Lieutenant Byron Rowles, and a servant to carry the terribly injured man to the beach at Stokes Bay where he was put aboard the yacht *Dream* and carried round to the Quebec Hotel at Old Portsmouth where attempts were made to save him. The wound was tended but the ball had carried with it powder, grease, and fragments of dirty wadding, the vital ingredients of severe infection. On 1 June, after eleven days of agony, Seton lost his battle with life. Two days later the coroner brought in a verdict of wilful murder. Hawkey and Pym stayed hidden until February of the next year, when Pym surrendered himself to the police. The following month he appeared at the Hampshire Assizes where a three-hour address from his counsel, Mr Serjeant Cockburn, swayed the jury and Pym was acquitted of the lesser charge of aiding and abbetting in the death of Seton. Before the trial had ended it was announced that Hawkey had come out of hiding and given himself up. He appeared at the next session of the assizes, supported by the same defence counsel, and he too was acquitted. In the aftermath of the trial public feeling ran so high that it became obvious that any future duelling would be dealt with very seriously, a pledge supported strongly by no less a political figure than the Duke of Wellington. After that tragic teatime meeting men were never again to duel on English soil to satisfy personal honour – so perhaps Captain James Alexander Seton did not die in vain.

The King's Rooms at Southsea where the far-reaching argument took place.

PROTECTION ABOUNDS

Where else in the world could you find a city completely protected by a ring of huge forts, none of which have ever fired a shot in anger? The giant defences which march along the top of Portsdown Hill, around to the coast at Gosport, and then out to sea like a giant's stepping stones, were the brainchild of Victorian prime minister Lord Palmerston as a defence against the threat from the French, who by this time had guns with rifled barrels which gave them greater accuracy and fire power. Palmerston had called for a royal commission to examine the question of the country's defence, and from that report the construction of the forts came about. In the

Fort Purbrook in the thirties.

Fort Nelson now houses a Royal Armouries exhibition.

event the French threat declined, and the forts forever became known as Palmerston's folly. It was thought the French would land elsewhere and reach Portsmouth from the north, so the forts were constructed to face outwards. From the south they are a familiar sight, but from the north they are all but invisible. Fort Elson and Fort Gomer at Gosport had already been built, so the new defences were added to the line. Fort Purbrook, Fort Widley, Fort Southwick, Fort Nelson, and Fort Wallington were built along the ridge of Portsdown, and each cost nearly £100,000 apiece. To protect the western approaches Fort Fareham, Fort Brockhurst, Fort Rowner and Fort Grange were added to the list. And in the Solent four free-standing forts were built to foil any approach from the sea. These were Spit Bank, No Man's Land, Horse Sand, and the tiny St Helen's huddled in the lee of Bembridge Harbour. Most of the land forts still stand. Fort Brockhurst is open to the public, as is Fort Nelson with its impressive collection of armoury. Fort Widley is owned by Portsmouth City Council and is open on certain days of the year, while Fort Purbrook houses a young people's activity centre.

Horse Sand Fort in unusual livery.

DOCKING

ack in 1494 Henry VII decided the town's destiny as a premier naval port when he commanded the construction of a dry dock – the first ever known in this country. Henry, who ascended the throne in 1485 following the defeat of Richard III at Bosworth, was the first of the Tudor line of rulers. He very soon appreciated the enviable position of Portsmouth as a naval base, and he began to build on this fact and improved the fortifications by building the Square Tower, still to be seen at Old Portsmouth. The work commenced in June 1495 and took forty-six weeks, at a total cost of £193. The main body of the dock was made of timber, which was then backfilled with 664 tons of stone and gravel. Four tons of iron were converted into spikes, bars and bolts, most of the work being undertaken at the forge which was set up on the site, and there were two sets of gates constructed from nearly 5000 feet of sawn timber planking. The first ship to enter the dock was the 600-ton *Sovereign*, which made history on 25 May, 1496. The ship's crew together with 120 labourers

*Henry VII,
dry dock builder.*

worked for 'a day and a night' to bring the vessel into the dock, and to fill the space between the two sets of gates with what was described as clay and rubbish. The *Sovereign* remained in the dock for eight months, and then the task of getting her out had to be faced. Twenty men worked for twenty-nine days in 'breking up of the dokke hede at every tide both day and night' and removing the tons of material from between the gates. No one really knows how the king came by the idea of a dry dock, but it certainly put Portsmouth on the naval map for the future.

PRESS PHOTOGRAPHER EXTRAORDINARY

Everyone must be familiar with the poster showing the grim features of Lord Kitchener used in the First World War to exhort everyone to join up with the declaration 'Your Country Needs You.' This hero of Khartoum never smiled in public, until he crossed the path of a Portsmouth man who claimed to be the country's first press photographer, Stephen Cribb. Cribb would go to almost any lengths to capture a good picture, and on one occasion when Kitchener was visiting the town, he clambered up garden wall to gain a good viewpoint. But the long arm of the law intervened and a policemen grabbed his leg in an attempt to dislodge him. As the struggle ensued, Kitchener became amused. The more the photographer clung grimly to the wall, the wider Kitchener's smile became – and Cribb, still clinging on for dear life, captured the moment on film. Such a rare picture proved to be a great money-spinner for the Portsmouth photographer who sold it as a postcard. Stephen Cribb was born in 1876, and began his photographic career in 1893, working for Mills in The Arcade, off Edinburgh Road. Later he went into business for himself in St Andrew's Road, Southsea, specialising in naval pictures and local events. His photographic skills became known worldwide, and Edward VII always insisted Cribb was on hand whenever he came to Portsmouth. He was a leader in the field of football photography, and was associated with Pompey all his life. He was a director in 1919 and was club chairman in 1945-46. His pictures were reproduced world wide and became so well known that at the height of his distinguished career letters addressed 'Cribb, England' reached him without delay. Stephen Cribb died in 1963 at the age of 87.

Kitchener is all smiles on Cribb's popular postcard.

Photographer extraordinary Stephen Cribb.

FULL STEAM AHEAD

In Victorian times supremacy of the sea was all important. The government firmly believed that a powerful navy would help preserve the British empire, so battleship building was big business. By the late 1890s Portsmouth was laying down at least one battleship a year. In 1891 Queen Victoria launched the battleship *Royal Sovereign*, which was commissioned in May 1892, only two years and eight months after the keel was laid, and four months ahead of schedule. This success was mainly due to one man – the Admiral Superintendent of the Dockyard, Jackie Fisher. In 1905 he became first sea lord, and began his drive to produce a brand-new design of warship with which to lead the world. *HMS Dreadnought*, the first of a new class, was laid down on 2 October, 1905, and with Fisher's demonic energy fuelling the work, she was launched by Edward VII on 10 February the following year after a mere 130 days. *Dreadnought* was the first battleship to cost in excess of £1m. She sailed for her sea trials in October 1906, just one year and a day after her keel was laid. It was said at the time that nowhere else in the world could such a feat have been possible, which puts Portsmouth well and truly into the shipbuilding firsts.

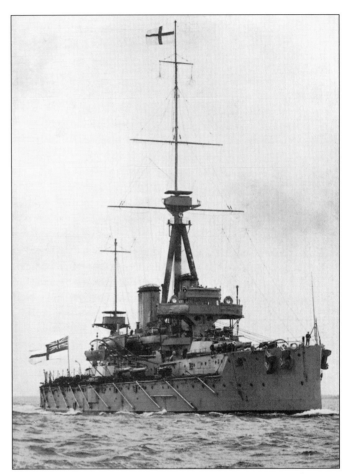

An evocative view of the huge HMS Dreadnought *taken by Portsmouth photographer Stephen Cribb.*

MARITIME MARVELS

I saw three ships on Christmas Day, says the old song. At Portsmouth's historic dockyard you can see three famous ships on every day but Christmas Day. The city's historic dockyard is home to a trio of historic vessels with a total age of more than 860 years. The baby of the bunch is the *Warrior*, whose masts dominate the skyline at the dockyard entrance in her berth near the South Railway jetty. On 16 June, 1987, crowds lined the shore to see the huge vessel return after a £7m restoration programme at Hartlepool. *Warrior* was the navy's first ironclad and was based at Portsmouth for most of her life. She was launched in 1860 and with her massive armament and armour plating she was the pride of the Victorian navy, but she never fired a shot in anger. She later became a torpedo training hulk in Portsmouth, and then a floating jetty at Milford Haven, from where

Mary Rose *is lifted from the seabed in the historic operation.*

she was rescued. Further inside the dockyard is *HMS Victory*, Nelson's flagship at Trafalgar. She was laid down in 1759 and was launched in 1765. After Trafalgar she returned to Portsmouth where she was a familiar sight in the harbour until 1922, when she was moved to her present resting place in dry dock. After painstaking restoration work she was finally returned to her condition as at Trafalgar, and in 1924 George V visited the old ship, officially marking the completion of the mammoth task. And the grand old lady of the trio is the *Mary Rose*, raised from the waters of the Solent in October 1982.

The ill-fated Tudor warship was built in 1511, but in 1545 she went down with nearly all hands in the waters off Southsea Castle, watched by Henry VIII. She was the flagship of a fleet assembled to combat the French fleet. She was raised in an historic operation and is now housed in the magnificent ship hall where visitors can hear about life aboard a Tudor warship, and can see the exhibition of artefacts brought up from the ship. Over the seventeen-year project to raise her, members of the team made 24,640 dives, and spent more than nine man-years under water.

Trafalgar veteran **HMS Victory** *between the wars dressed overall for Empire Day.*

Spectators gather at
The Hard as
Warrior *is eased*
towards her
permanent berth.

SAILING INTO HISTORY

Back in 1967 a Southsea greengrocer went into the history books with a daring exploit. On 16 July of that year former naval lieutenant Alec Rose started off in his tiny yacht *Lively Lady* on his second attempt to sail round the world single handed. He had started off on a similar bid the year before, but had run into a string of problems, including being run down in the Atlantic by an unidentified cargo vessel. This time he was more fortunate, and when he made landfall in Australia, he was telephoned by the lord mayor of Portsmouth who told him he was to be made a Freeman of the city. He finally arrived back in his home port on 4 July, 1968, to a tremendous welcome from residents and visitors alike. Hundreds of craft followed him in on his last leg down to Spithead, and following landfall he was driven to the Guildhall in a convertible Rolls-Royce with the registration number AR1. The next day he received the news that he was to be knighted, bringing royal approval for a real man of Portsmouth. *Lively Lady* can be seen moored near the Boardwalk at the Port Solent marina.

Sir Alec Rose

Alec Rose's **Lively Lady** *berthed at Port Solent marina.*

Flashback to July 1968 and crowds cheer Alec Rose as he travels to the Guildhall in an open car after his epic voyage.

THE FIRST NELSON'S COLUMN

High on the crest of Portsdown Hill, at a point where the ancient track from Portchester to Southwick crossed the ridge, stands the other Nelson's Column. It is 120 feet high and its base is 300 feet above sea level, and in early days it became a beacon for ships at Spithead. The tiny bust of Nelson sits at the top, protected by a stone hood, and the base has an Egyptian look, perhaps a reminder of one of the great admiral's famous triumphs – the Battle of the Nile. The pillar was erected in 1807, two years after Trafalgar, and, as the famous London landmark wasn't completed until 1843, this surely makes Portsmouth's structure the FIRST Nelson's Column.

Nelson solemnly looks down on Portsmouth from his vantage point on the crest of Portsdown Hill.

THE BIRTHPLACE OF AUSTRALIA

Portsmouth's claim to be the birthplace of Australia was cemented in spectacular fashion on 13 May, 1987, when the Queen and the Duke of Edinburgh visited the city as part of a colourful series of events to commemorate Australia's bicentenary.

Aboriginal dancers and marching bands entertained a huge crowd in the Guildhall Square, and the day ended with a re-enactment of the departure of the first convict fleet, which sailed from Portsmouth on 13 May, 1787. To mark the link the Queen unveiled a plaque at Sally Port.

Hundreds of balloons fill the air over the Guildhall Square at the launch of the celebrations in 1987.

WIDOW'S COURAGEOUS CHALLENGE

A memorial in St Mary's churchyard tells a story of courage, and of how a Portsmouth family put its name on the world map for posterity. The tall obelisk beneath the trees in the grounds of the Fratton church recalls the Revd William Bussell, a former curate at St Mary's who died in 1820, leaving a widow and eight children. The young mother faced the daunting task of feeding and educating her brood, and eventually

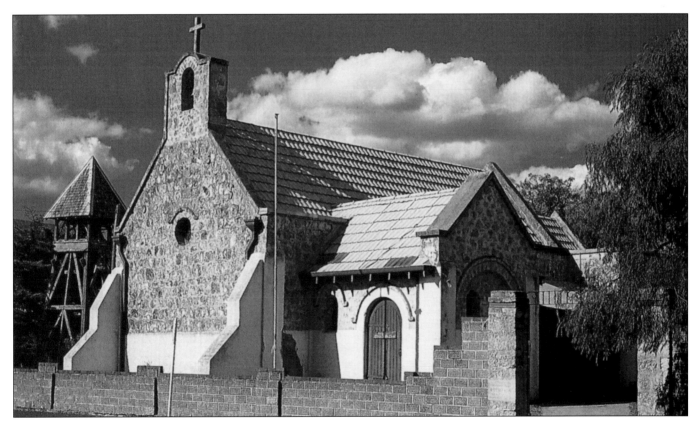

St Mary's church, Busselton – the oldest stone-built church in Western Australia.

after a few years of hardship the family decided to take the plunge and emigrate to Australia and start a new life. They plumped for Western Australia, then only thinly populated around Perth, and in 1830 the four eldest brothers, John, Charles, Vernon, and Alfred, arrived and set up their pioneering settlement. By the time the rest of the family arrived three years later a small community had established itself around the Bussells' homestead. They had taken wheat seeds with them from Portsmouth and by 1836 they produced enough surplus to sell or to trade for other goods, and so the beginning of the Australian wheat belt was established. The settlement meanwhile was growing, and the name Busselton was adopted for this new and thriving township. Busselton now is a popular seaside resort, but the link with the homeland is still there. On the wall in the town's St Mary's church is a plaque commemorating the Revd William Bussell and the pioneering family that took Portsmouth to the new world.

The memorial to the Revd William Bussell in the grounds of St Mary's church, Portsmouth.

POOR BOY'S SUCCESS DOWN UNDER

What is the link between a huge rock formation in the Uluru National Park in Western Australia and a Portsmouth school? The distinctive Ayers Rock is a great tourist attraction to visitors and is a sacred place to the aborigines, and in 1883 was given its name in honour of a Portsmouth-born man. And the old Beneficial School, now the Beneficial Centre, in Kent Street, is the link with Down Under. Back in 1754 eight philanthropic men met and formed the Beneficial Society, with the main aim of educating poor children. A parcel of land was bought for £280 and the two-storey building was constructed, with the school rooms on the ground floor and society meeting rooms above. Many deserving youngsters were given a head start in life at what was known as, 'Old Benny,' and one who went a long way to make his name in the world was Henry Ayers. Henry Ayers was born in 1821, the son of dockyard worker William Ayers and his wife Elizabeth. In 1832 he entered the legal office of S.W. Blyth at Portsea, and in June 1840 married Anne Potts at Alverstoke. Within weeks Henry, his new wife, and her family had embarked aboard the *Fairfield* bound for Australia. Tragedy hit them on the trip for Henry's new mother-in-law had died by the time the ship had reached Cape Town. They carried on, however, and the shipping list shows their arrival as 14 December, 1840. Eleven days after landfall Henry joined Mr J. H. Richman in his Adelaide firm of solicitors, where he worked for some years. However it was the discovery of copper at Burra Burra in 1845, and his shrewd investment in the mine, that made Henry Ayers a rich man. He began his politi-

Sir Henry Ayers – pioneer and businessman.

cal career on 9 March 1857 when he was elected a member of the legislative council in Adelaide, a position he retained for 36 years. He served as president of the assembly for 12 years, and was seven times premier of South Australia. In 1883 explorer and surveyor William Gosse paid tribute to him by naming Ayers Rock in his honour. Henry never forgot his beginnings in Portsmouth and his days at the school. In 1878 he wrote to headmaster James Slade offering a donation and asking to become an honorary member of the Beneficial Society. James Slade was the son of Thomas Slade, the school's longest-serving and most effective headmaster.

The Beneficial Centre today.

The old Beneficial School where Henry Ayers was a pupil.

DICKENS OF A GOOD READ

Although Charles Dickens lived in Portsmouth for just a short while after his birth, his name will forever be associated with the city. Dickens was born on 2 February, 1812, at 1 Mile End Terrace, Landport, which had been home to the family since 1809, although the address now is 393 Old Commercial Road. By the summer of 1812 the family had moved to less expensive accommodation at 16

Charles Dickens's birthplace, a museum in what is now a pretty conservation area.

Hawke Street, Portsea, and later to Wish Street, Southsea, returning eventually to London in 1814, before moving to Chatham in Kent. Dickens's father was a clerk in the Royal Navy pay office, but the family was seldom free of financial distress. At the age of nine the young Charles was sent to work in a blacking warehouse. By the time he was fifteen he obtained a position as an office boy, and later got a job as a reporter. In 1834 his first piece of fiction, one of the *Sketches by Boz* series, was published, and two years later, when he was just twenty four, the first of the *Pickwick Papers* saw the light of day and his reputation was assured. He returned to the town in 1858 and again in 1866, when he visited Mile End Terrace, but was unable to identify his actual birthplace. Today a plaque can be seen on the wall of the Hawke Street house, marking the Dickens family's time there.

Charles Dickens.

THE DICKENS CONNECTION

The Highland Cemetery at Southsea has already proved to be the resting place of many of this country's heroes, but it also boasts a virtual encyclopedia of connections with Charles Dickens. Just past a small monkey puzzle tree – there to prevent the Devil seeing who was being buried – is the last resting place of Maria Winter, née Beadnall, the first sweetheart of Dickens, whose love went unrequited. And a few yards away lies Ellen Robinson, née Ternan, who was Dickens's mistress. Recently the two graves were rededicated by the Dickens Fellowship based at Portsmouth University. Nearby is the grave of Georgina Margaret Hayman, on whom Dickens is believed to have based his famous character, Little Dorrit. The solicitor father of the then Georgina Bridges was a close friend of the great author, and he knew the young girl well. The Bridges family also had a son who was crippled after falling on park railings, and Dickens based his Tiny Tim character on him. Unlike his literary counterpart the young boy died in his teens. And the Dickensian group is completed by the grave of Alfred Arthur Seale, first curator of the Charles Dickens Museum in Portsmouth. The cemetery was first opened in 1852 as the Portsea Island Cemetery, and was created because the graveyard at St Thomas's church, now Portsmouth Cathedral, was running out of space.

Little Dorrit's grave at Highland Cemetery.

BUBBLES

In 1943 and 1944 the member of parliament for Portsmouth North was Admiral Sir William James. Admiral James was a highly-decorated naval veteran who had joined the service during Victoria's reign, serving aboard one of the last sailing vessels in the Royal Navy. During the Great War he served with the Grand Fleet in the battle crusier *HMS Queen Mary*, but fortunately left the ship just before she was sunk in the Battle of Jutland on 31 May, 1916. He was subsequently appointed flag commander in the 4th Battle Squadron. From 1923 to 1925 he was deputy director of the Royal Naval Staff College at Greenwich, becoming director in 1925. He was promoted to flag rank in 1929 and was lord commissioner of the Admiralty and deputy chief of naval staff from 1935 to 1938, when at the outbreak of the Second World War was promoted to full admiral and became commander-in-chief, Portsmouth. From 1943 to 1944 he was chief of naval information, and while in this civilian post he became an MP. Upon his retirement in 1942 Admiral James was made a Freeman of Portsmouth. He was created KCB in 1936 and GCB in 1944. However important these facts are to naval historians and students of politics, Admiral Sir William James's picture would have been seen by almost everyone in the country for an entirely different reason. To tell the story we must go back to about 1886 when William James was a curly-haired lad of about five. His grandfather, the eminent and prodigious Pre-Raphaelite painter Sir John Millais, used the boy as a model for a painting called 'A Child's World'. It depicted the lad sitting on a box blowing bubbles from a clay pipe.

Admiral William James.

The painting was first shown at the Royal Academy, but it was later reproduced in the *Illustrated London News*, who had bought the painting. Then Thomas Barratt, the far-sighted partner in the Pears Soap Company, saw the sales potential of the picture. He subsequently bought it for 2000 guineas, commissioned an artist to paint a bar of Pears soap in the bottom right-hand corner, and renamed the painting 'Bubbles'. The distinctive trademark was used on posters and advertisements, and hundreds of thousands of postcards were given away in stores when the Pears travelling roadshow came to town. Although Millais was displeased at the thought of his creation being used for advertising he gradually mellowed and warmed to the idea. There are also other local links with 'Bubbles'. The James family had connections with Turret House at Portchester, and local legend has it that the study was painted in the village. And some residents say the clay pipe in the picture is similar to those made at the old Portchester factory. But in reality all the signs place the picture's creation in London. The James family was living in the capital at the time where William's father was at the War Office, and Southampton-born Millais was known to have visited them. Millais was in the process of painting the picture in November 1885, and during this time wrote to Beatrix Potter's father – a keen photographer – asking for his help with studies of soap bubbles. At this time Millais had his studio in Palace Gate, Kensington. But wherever 'Bubbles' was painted it made William James arguably the most famous boy in the country.

The famous 'Bubbles' painting with the bar of Pears soap in the bottom corner.

RIDING INTO THE RECORD BOOKS

At the turn of the century cycling was riding high in the popularity polls, and clubs catering for the beginner and the expert alike sprang up all over the country. And in 1908 it was a Portsmouth racing cyclist who took the honours at the world's most prestigious event – the Olympic Games. The young Clarence Brickwood Kingsbury took two gold medals at the games, held at the White City, London, beating off the best riders from France and Italy, both countries with a great cycling tradition. But having gained the two golds Kingsbury had to leave immediately for the World Championships in Leipzig, Germany, so his daughter deputised for him at the ceremony, accepting the award from Queen Alexandra. On his return to Portsmouth, thousands of well-wishers lined the streets to cheer as he made his way to the town hall square, where it was said more than 15,000 people had gathered. Later in the day a concert featuring stars from the New Hippodrome Theatre was held in his honour at the Masonic Hall, Lake Road. Kingsbury continued racing for several more years winning many more events, and his daughters, Leonie and Thelma, carried on the family sporting tradition to become leading British badminton and tennis champions. Clarence Kingsbury died on 4 March, 1949, at his Southsea home, leaving golden memories of his sporting prowess. The city museum holds some Kingsbury memorabilia, including his gold medals and cap.

Cycling legend Clarence Kingsbury.

SEVENTEEN SHILLINGS – THE PRICE OF FAME

In the thirties and forties before the advent of television, radio was the entertainment medium of most households. To hear the voices of wireless celebrities coming into their homes was a great delight for most listeners, and many stars became thought of as family friends. The then director general of the BBC, John Reith, firmly believed that the medium of radio should educate as well as entertain, and programmes such as the *Brains Trust*, which answered questions sent in by listeners, were very popular. And one of the most popular of the experts featured regularly on that programme was Professor Joad. Cyril Edwin Mitchinson Joad joined the programme in 1941 when it was part of the question-and-answer series *Any Questions*. The series changed its title to the *Brains Trust* on 4 January, 1942. Joad the philosopher and prolific author became a stalwart of the programme, and his cautionary preface to an answer: 'It depends what you mean by ...' became a national catchphrase. He became known as the Plato of the pubs, and his statements were argued about and discussed in bars, around kitchen tables, and in thousands of living rooms. Although not a true son of Portsmouth, Cyril Joad lived for a great deal of his life at Clarence Parade, Southsea, where his mother, May, kept a private hotel. His father, Edwin, a past chairman of the Portsmouth Literary and Scientific Society, was inspector of schools for Hampshire. Cyril Joad was educated at Blundell's School, Tiverton, and went with a scholarship to Oxford where he took a first in Greats. From there he went into the civil service but in 1930 resigned to become head of the department of philosophy and psychology at Birkbeck College, London. However, sadly, it was Lord Reith's puritan rule of the BBC, combined with Joad's philosophy of life, which led to the radio professor's downfall. In his time on the air he said many audacious things. One of them was that in one respect he was a criminal – he liked travelling first class on the railway with only a third-class ticket. 'There is the thrill of anticipation and apprehension, wondering whether one is going to get caught,' he once said. And on 5 January 1948 he WAS caught, on an Exeter-bound train. He had neither a third-class ticket nor any other kind, and had been trying to save himself 17s 1d. He was fined 40 shillings with 25 guineas costs, and within hours had been dropped by the BBC, becoming a *Brains Trust* back number. He retired to his farm near Midhurst, Sussex, and eventually died in April 1953 after a long illness.

Professor Cyril Joad, Brains Trust *stalwart*.

SHIPPING INTELLIGENCE

A young late-Victorian artist with an inexhaustable fund of enthusiasm and a capacity for taking pains started to compile an album of warship drawings. Fred T. Jane's ambition was to include every type of armoured warship afloat, and the title selected was *Ironclads of the World*. Such an undertaking presented a formidable task to the young man as the only data concerning foreign ships was the crude outline plans in a few naval reference books. As the years progressed Jane added to his store of information, but his greatest piece of good fortune was to meet W. A. Bieber who possessed what was possibly the finest collection of warship photographs then in existence, which he placed at Jane's disposal. By 1897 the first edition of what has become known as the sailor's bible came off the presses. *All the World's Fighting Ships* was priced at 10s 6d (52p),and met with such an enthusiastic reception that it had to be reprinted the following year, and Jane's reputation was made. Although not a native of Portsmouth, Jane lived in the town for most of his life, and during his time became well known for his many articles in the *Hampshire Telegraph*, his work with the local scouting movement, his powerful cars, and his continual fight to convince the government that the 12mph speed limit was

Fred T. Jane plans his strategy for Jane's Fighting Ships.

too low. He also had aspirations to become a pioneer aviator, building a miniplane which, although innovative, sadly was unsuccessful. He died at his home in Elphinstone Road, Southsea, in March 1916. *Jane's Fighting Ships* and its various offshoots has been published continuously for 100 years, and Jane's name has become part of maritime history.

SPIRIT OF CO-OPERATION

It has always been assumed that the co-operative movement had its beginnings in Toad Lane, Rochdale, in 1840, when cotton workers bought flour and sold it to their colleagues at advantageous rates. But suprisingly, forty-four years earlier, a similar scheme had been launched in Portsmouth, making it possibly the earliest co-operative society in England. In 1796 a group of dockyard men banded together to form the Union Society, with the object of building a windmill and a bakery to produce cheaper bread for their members and customers. The money was raised by shares, subscribed to by the 880 members according to their position in the yard. Craftsmen paid in six shillings a quarter, and labourers four shillings, until such time that the required amount was raised and the mill was built. However sixteen years into the new century there were plans afoot to enlarge the dockyard, and the Union Society was forced to move. They realised their assets, sold the mill to the government, and formed a new co-operative, the Dock Mill Society. With the money they bought land at Southsea and built a new mill and a block of six cottages. The Dock Mill was built by the dockyard workers, for which they bought a million bricks from the government Board of Ordnance, each stamped with the broad arrow. The mill was 100 feet high, surrounded by a balcony of nearly 200 feet in circumference, and boasted sails with a span of 80 feet. In 1815 the society, encouraged by the success of the mill, opened a brewery, which was sadly a failure and was sold in 1819. By 1834 the depression following the Napoleonic wars had lifted, wages rose, and the price of flour and bread decreased. The society was unable to compete and finally went into liquidation. The mill itself stayed derelict for another forty years until it was bought by enterprising miller Maurice Welch, who worked it until 1923 when he closed it. The structure was subsequently demolished but the restored cottages remain on the site at Napier Road, the only memento of an experiment that was ahead of its time.

The Dock Mill at Southsea in its heyday.

HELPING YOURSELF

A later co-operative movement in Portsmouth also boasted another first. The Portsea Island Mutual Co-operative Society was formed in 1873 in a rented shop in Charles Street, Portsea.

Trading was done only during the evening hours, when butter, tea, flour and sugar were sold to its members at discounted rates. Within a year membership had grown along with demand, and the shop, which moved to larger

The interior of the shop in Albert Road – the first self-service store in the country.

premises in Curtis Terrace, opened during the day. In June 1878 it was decided that rented premises were inadequate, so a plot at Besant Road was bought for £75, a £300 mortgage was obtained, and a new store was built. Other branches opened in Buckland and St James's Road in 1882, and from small beginnings the huge shopping empire began to spread. Shoppers were encouraged to join the society and to benefit from dividend on purchases, and gradually the society membership list grew, eventually leading to the vast company we know today.

The Portsea Island Co-op has always been innovative, but is was in 1948 that the society took an important step and introduced a completely new kind of shopping. It launched the first totally self-service store in the United Kingdom, in Albert Road, Southsea. It was an immediate success, and within two months trade at the branch had increased by 80 per cent. By the end of the year the society had opened four more self-service branches, and soon other societies had followed suit, leading to the present-day supermarkets and superstores.

DIVING INTO HISTORY

Portsmouth Swimming Club was founded in 1875. It was later to become the largest of its kind in the country and boasted nearly 1500 members. Summer visitors could use the facilities for a nominal charge. The club's wooden bathing stages – separate ones for men and women – were situated near Clarence Pier

The ladies' bathing stage was separated from that of the men.

BACCY AND SPUDS

In July of 1586 an expedition sent out to Virginia by Sir Walter Raleigh arrived in Portsmouth. The leader, Ralph Lane, brought with him something never seen before in England, and which was to have an important effect on the future life of British people – tobacco. While away many of the crewmen had adopted smoking, but when they were seen walking in the streets of Portsmouth with their pipes it caused great consternation among the residents. As well as tobacco, Lane is supposed to have brought potatoes into England for the first time, and also through the port of Portsmouth. Lane was knighted by Queen Elizabeth I for his services to the country and in 1588 was made governor of Southsea Castle. Portsmouth had already scored a first in the reign of Edward III when a ship arrived in the port carrying a cargo of Spanish oranges – a fruit never before seen in this country. The king swiftly travelled to Portsmouth and bought the entire shipment for his queen to remind her of her Castilian home. It is also believed that bananas were first brought to England through Portsmouth, which eventually led one of the country's largest importers, Fyffes, to set up its base here.

Sir Walter Raleigh.

NO HOPE FROM WARTIME LEGACY

Portsmouth is a proud old city, and during the last war she stood up to the might of the German bombing. On one fateful night, 10 January 1941, huge areas of the city were laid waste and Clarence Pier and the Hippodrome Theatre disappeared from the city's map forever. Gradually the regeneration of Portsmouth saw the bomb sites cleared, and by 1984 only one remained – that of the old Hippodrome in what is now Guildhall Walk. And on one fateful day – 12 October 1984 – the old theatre decided to get into the limelight again, puting her more modern neighbour into darkness. Earlier that day the Guildhall had been buzzing as the preparations for a stage scoop were under way. American entertainer and comedian Bob Hope was to appear, one of only a few dates he was to make in the country of his birth. But by lunchtime all that was to change. A digger driver working on the site of the old Hippodrome dug up what he thought was a milk churn. But closer inspection revealed that the unwelcome visitor was a huge 500lb German bomb, which had lain undisturbed since 1941. Within minutes the police had sealed off the area and thousands of workers were evacuated from offices, shops, and more importantly from the Guildhall. By 2.30pm a bomb disposal squad had arrived from Chatham and the delicate work of steaming out the explosive and making the bomb safe began – a job which was to continue until 5.00 the next morning. Portsmouth City Council chief executive Richard Trist had the unenviable job of informing the surprised Mr Hope on his arrival at Portsmouth station that his engagement had been cancelled because of the wartime legacy. Bob Hope had spent many hours at the front entertaining the troops at many theatres of war, but Portsmouth was the first to black out the show even before it had started.

Chief Executive Richard Trist tells a shocked Bob Hope that his concert has been cancelled.

Bomb disposal team members steam out the explosive from the 500lb bomb.

GUNWHARF

The Gunwharf was originally an army base but was taken over by the Navy in 1923 where it housed the Torpedo School HMS Vernon. The view today would be completely different to that shown in the picture, which was taken in about 1995. Now the area is a mecca for visitors with shops, bars and restaurants to tempt all choices. Gunwharf is also home to Portsmouth's newst 'first,' the 557ft-high Spinnaker Tower, which provides unrivalled panoramic views from its observation decks.

ABOUT THE AUTHOR

Anthony Triggs is the author of 14 previous books on the history of the Portsmouth area, including *Sunny Southsea* and *Portsmouth: the Shattered City* for Halsgrove. He is a retired journalist and lives at Portchester with his wife Sue. In addition to his interest in local history, Anthony is a keen family historian.